Contents

WHAT IS MENTAL HEALTH?

*M*ental health often gets mixed up with mental illness, but mental illness is not the same as mental health.

Our mental health is to do with how we think and feel about ourselves, the world around us and other people.

It's to do with how we manage really big feelings, how we get on with each other, how we make choices, how we handle stressful situations and what we do. It's linked to our physical health too.

Mental health is our *"emotional, psychological, and social well-being"*.
(World Health Organisation)

"Mental health is just health."
(Matt Haig, author)

Mental health is a spectrum

Our physical health can range from us feeling terrible to feeling great, and everything in between. Our mental health can do this too.

Sometimes we might feel really on top of things and comfortable in who we are – as if we could handle anything.

Other times we might feel extremely scared or upset, or find it hard to think clearly. We might feel very alone.

If we feel really sad or frightened like this it can make it hard to cope with everyday life and do the things we want to do.

This book is about the whole range of mental health, from feeling good and being able to do what we like, to needing extra help with thoughts or feelings or behaviours that have got out of hand.

Who has mental health?

EVERYONE has mental health. It's really important that we look after our mental health and the mental health of those around us.

> *"It's about all of us taking responsibility for our happiness and our mental well-being as a community. I think we need to stop thinking about it as a quarter of people over there who need to sort themselves out."*
>
> Natasha Devon, writer and mental health advocate

Mental health and feelings

Having good mental health doesn't mean being happy all the time. No one only feels happy. Different feelings are useful to get us to do things and to help us understand things that happen. Strong feelings aren't bad.

Sometimes it might feel like our feelings are being blown about by the wind. We might wake up one day feeling really grumpy, and then later on feel happy. We might wake up in the night feeling scared, and then in the morning can't imagine how strong that worry was.

Feelings are a bit like the weather, they come and go. One thing that's certain is that they will change, though sometimes it takes a while.

This book explains what mental health is, where it comes from, things that can help us to look after it, things that might make it feel worse, and support we can get if we feel we're struggling. It includes different people's points of view, from quotes that people have said about mental health to pieces of writing that people have contributed especially for the book.

You don't have to read it all in one go, you can dip in and out if you want to. Sometimes there are 'think abouts', asking you to consider your viewpoint on different issues.

How are mental and physical health related?

Our mental health and our physical health affect each other. It's not surprising really, because most processes to do with our emotions and thoughts happen in our brain, which is part of our body.

Exercise, eating well, getting enough sleep, and taking time to rest are all things that are important for our mental health as well as our physical health. So in that way it's win-win, these things are good for us all over.

Research into links between our gut and our brain shows that we are only just beginning to understand how healthy eating can boost how we feel.

Stress impacts on our mental health, and it can also have physical effects. Some physical health conditions can be associated with stress, and some physical symptoms can be helped by relieving stress.

If we are physically healthy we can do more things we want to do and we usually feel happier. If we are physically unwell or have a physical disability then this might get in the way of what we want to do and we might feel sad, anxious or frustrated.

Having a physical illness or disability increases the risk of mental health problems, although this doesn't mean that someone with a physical health problem will always have a mental health problem.

Mental health problems

Having a mental health problem or a difficulty doesn't mean anything bad or different about someone as a person, it's part of the range of human experiences that any of us could have.

Sometimes people struggle for a bit with something and then go back to feeling fine; other times people learn to live alongside a mental health problem for longer. Either way there is help available and it's good to talk about how we feel.

Mental health problems can feel frightening, and sometimes I think that fear can become catching. Other people can feel afraid or awkward around someone with a mental illness, or worry that talking will make it worse. I think this is a shame. Asking how people are can help.

Why even more support should be available

Mental health is often talked about by politicians, but the funding that mental health services get is very far behind physical health services.

Mental health can also relate to school stresses, such as teachers and students being rated on test and exam scores. Schools need enough funding and enough freedom to look after how young people feel as well as how they do in exams.

Mental health can also relate to how things are at home for children. Social care services need enough funding to be able to support families.

What does good mental health feel like?

When our mental health is good we feel okay about ourselves and who we are for most of the time. We are able to make and keep friendships. When we experience stressful things we feel able to cope. We might feel sad sometimes but this feeling doesn't hang around and it doesn't make us so upset that we can't do the stuff we want to do. We are able to learn and grow and change and make decisions, and enjoy life.

> *"Being completely involved in an activity for its own sake... Time flies. Every action, movement, and thought follows inevitably from the previous one ..."*
>
> Mihaly Csikszentmihalyi, psychologist

This quote describes what the psychologist Mihaly Csikszentmihalyi called "flow" and is the feeling often described by musicians, dancers and sports people when they are doing what they love.

THINK ABOUT

What things do you do that make you feel happy, calm and contented? Or that make you feel in a state of "flow"?

My Experience

LUCY MADDOX

Who I am and what I do

My name's Lucy. I live in Bristol and I work as a clinical psychologist and writer.

Being a clinical psychologist means that I have been trained in talking therapies, to help with different sorts of mental health problems. The training also taught me about research, and about how we can use evidence to see what is most helpful.

Lots of my work has been in mental health wards for teenagers who are having a really tough time. I now work with foster carers, helping them to think about how best to look after young people who have come from difficult backgrounds. I also work one-to-one with young people and with adults.

I try to help people to explore and understand what is going on for them or for the children they care for, what might be keeping problems going, and what might help.

I sometimes use a structure like this to guide conversations ⟶

Why me?
Longer-term things that may have made the problem more likely

Why now?
Triggers?

Whats up?
What's the problem?

Why still?
What keeps the problem going?

What helps?

I love sharing psychology ideas. I write about psychology and make a podcast called 'What is CBT?' about cognitive behavioural therapy. You can read more about CBT and other types of talking therapy later in this book.

Things that help my mental health

Being young can be stressful: I remember having worries and not knowing what to do. Just like there are things we can do to improve our physical health, there are also things we can do to improve our mental health. These will be different for each of us. For me they include having regular exercise, sleeping enough, spending time with people I love, making time for things I enjoy, being kind to myself if I make a mistake, trying not to get too busy, and trying to notice things I feel good about. Also hanging out with the cat.

Why I think it's helpful to learn about our mental health

Some things that affect our mental health are things we can control and others aren't. Things we can't control often include stressful situations or experiences. We also can't control whether or not we are genetically more vulnerable to having a mental health problem (but this doesn't mean that this is set in stone - it's to do with lots of different factors, there's more on this later).

There are other things that we can control. There are things that we can learn to look after in ourselves and for each other. There are useful skills that can boost our mental healthiness, and some of those are in this book. Being kind, to ourselves and to each other, is crucial.

"Being kind, to ourselves and to each other, is crucial."

WHAT ARE MENTAL HEALTH PROBLEMS?

We all have times when we feel sad, or worried, or confused, or when we get stuck thinking about the same thing over and over again. This doesn't mean we have a mental health problem.

Getting in the way of everyday life

Mental health problems (or mental illnesses) are when worries or feelings get a LOT bigger, to the point where they get in the way of our everyday life and cause us a lot of distress. They might make us do unusual things. We might not feel ourselves or we might experience unusual thoughts or sensations. We might find it hard to concentrate or to do the things we want to do.

For example, someone feeling sad sometimes but still being able to do things they enjoy is one thing, but feeling so sad that they can't get out of bed is different.

Or, hearing voices might not bother a person if they are occasional and not scary, but another person might hear them all the time, saying horrible things, and feel terrified.

Different sorts of problems

There are different names for different sorts of mental health problems, depending on which feelings or thoughts or behaviours have got really big - some examples are: depression, obsessive compulsive disorder, anxiety, psychosis, post-traumatic stress disorder, and eating disorders (there is more information about these in the glossary on page 47).

These diagnoses try to separate out different sorts of problems, with the aim of being able to treat them better. There can be quite a lot of overlap between diagnoses though. For example, depression and anxiety quite often happen together. There's also some debate about diagnoses which we'll come to later. Learning disabilities and learning difficulties like dyslexia are not mental health problems.

It isn't always easy to tell when our mental health will tip from feeling okay to feeling like we're really struggling. It usually involves a combination of lots of different things. That's one reason why it's helpful to have some healthy habits to keep us feeling as good as possible. There are lots of things we can do to look after our mental health.

Describing difficulties

Mental health problems can happen to anyone. Here's what different famous people have said about their experiences:

Winston Churchill (prime minister of the UK during the Second World War) apparently described low moods as being like a Black Dog.

"It's that cold absence of feeling - that really hollowed-out feeling."

JK Rowling, author, on depression

"When you're high it's tremendous. The ideas and feelings are fast and frequent like shooting stars, and you follow them until you find better and brighter ones ... But, somewhere, this changes. The fast ideas are far too fast, and there are far too many ... You are irritable, angry, frightened, uncontrollable, and enmeshed totally in the blackest caves of the mind ..."

Kay Redfield Jamison, clinical psychologist and writer, on bipolar disorder

"I started having panic attacks, and the scariest part was it could be triggered by anything. I used to cover my face with a pillow whenever I had to walk outside from the car to the studio."

Ellie Goulding, singer, on anxiety

"It was like a whirlwind for me."

Stormzy, rapper, on experiencing depression

My Experience

LIZ ATKIN

Who are you? How does your art relate to mental health?

My name is Liz Atkin and I am a visual artist based in London.

I have Compulsive Skin Picking, a mental health problem thought to affect one in 25 people. Individuals who struggle with this touch, rub, scratch, pick at or dig into their skin to manage stress or anxiety. Occasionally picking at the skin is a very common human behaviour. Compulsive skin picking, however, is in a family of body-focused repetitive behaviours, along with a hair pulling disorder (called trichotillomania) and other types of self-grooming, which are very hard to stop – and that can cause a lot of distress.

For more than 10 years I have been making artwork, including drawings, photographs and performances, to transform my experience of this illness and manage my wellbeing. I share my experience to raise awareness for the disorder around the world, and have exhibited and taught in the UK, Europe, Australia, USA, Singapore and Japan. I've given away more than 17,000 free #CompulsiveCharcoal newspaper drawings which I create and give to commuters on public transport in London, New York, San Francisco, Singapore, Cologne and elsewhere.

Compulsive charcoal drawings

Liz first drew on a discarded newspaper in October 2015 when she ran out of sketchbook on a journey from South to North London and wanted to avoid skin picking and experiencing a panic attack. Now, on average, she makes 60 of these drawings a day, often giving them away to commuters.

What does mental health mean to you?

We all have a brain as well as a body – we have physical and mental health. Mental illness is when we feel unwell emotionally. It's important to look after my wellbeing – my mental health - from day to day. Since anxiety and skin picking happen when I feel tense, worried or upset about something, I've found drawing helps me to channel the tense and uncomfortable energy into something mindful and creative.

Each and every mark on the paper is a moment to refocus my fingers and relax my mind. Drawing is very absorbing; the rhythmic repetitive motion of marks and smudges on paper is energising but also very soothing for me. I work with charcoal which is messy and the dust quickly covers my fingers; it prevents me from moving my hands to pick at the skin on my face or body. The touch and repetition of drawing has a very strong connection for me to the skin picking, my hands move fast; perhaps that is why it has become so effective – it calms anxiety and helps me feel better.

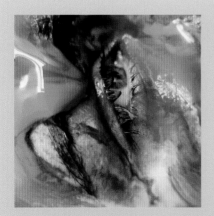

Do you have any advice for people reading this book?

We all have physical and mental health. All sorts of things can impact how we feel emotionally. It's always okay to ask for help or advice to talk about feelings or difficult experiences with someone we trust. Creative activities like drawing, painting, photography, acting, dance or music can be a great way to lift our mood, or express how we feel.

This painting is a self portrait called Resilience I.

"It's always okay to ask for help or advice to talk about feelings or difficult experiences with someone we trust."

HOW DO WE KNOW WHAT'S HEALTHY OR NOT?

What we think of as healthy or "normal" can change. At different times in history and in different places in the world, different things have been described as a mental illness.

I love this drawing by Edward Monkton. It's easy to get caught up in worrying about whether we are "normal". But actually, is being normal something helpful to aim for? We're all different, and our weirdnesses and quirkiness are what makes us who we are.

Changes over time

Identifying as gay used to be wrongly thought of as a mental illness. We now know that this is harmful and discriminatory. There might be other things we label as mental illness today that we might not in the future. It's important that we keep checking whether diagnoses are useful or harmful.

We've also changed the way we talk about mental health over time. People used to be called "mad". Often certain groups of people got called "mad" more than others, like women in the Victorian era, who were often labelled with "hysteria" and could be sent to an asylum by their male relatives. Often the treatment suggestion for a Victorian woman who had "hysteria" was to get married!

Why were more women than men diagnosed with hysteria in the Victorian era? Maybe women were more miserable because they had fewer rights? Maybe it was a way to ignore people who were upset about how they were being treated? Maybe it was because women didn't have the power to give diagnoses? It's important that we watch out for people being told they have a mental illness when actually they are trying to speak up about things they want to change.

Different ideas in different cultures

Hearing voices or having other unusual experiences is more common than is often thought, and there are different views about whether this is a mental health problem.

In many cultures, including Maori cultures in New Zealand, and Aboriginal cultures in Australia, it's not considered unusual to hear voices of family members who have died. In other cultures this might be labelled as a sign of mental illness.

Whether we label something as a mental health problem depends how much the experience gets in the way of our life and how much it upsets us.

Diagnoses pros and cons

Diagnoses are short-hand labels for groups of experiences. There are different ideas about diagnosis.

Some pros can be:

- helping people feel more understood and less alone
- being clear about what the problem is so we can try to help
- recognising the seriousness of the problem

"What's underestimated is the overwhelming relief people feel when they get a mental illness diagnosis."

Grace Vaughan, writer

Some cons can be:

- Feeling known as a diagnosis rather than as a person
- Feeling confused when diagnoses overlap
- Wider causes of a problem being overlooked

"I choose to live alongside my experiences, rather than suppress them with large doses of medication. To me, they are not symptoms — they are meaningful responses to a life that has thrown many challenges my way… I now hear more voices than ever, but I feel happy with the fact that they're my voices. They relate to my life … even if they feel very separate — and they're mine to deal with."

Rai Waddingham, trainer and consultant

WHERE DOES MENTAL HEALTH COME FROM?

There is not one thing that affects our mental health, there are lots of things. Some things are in our control and others aren't.

Some of the things are to do with people and events and environments around us: stresses, difficult things that happen, situations we are in and also sometimes things we choose to do.

*Some of the things are to do with our biology: our brain and our genes. One of the reasons why it's complicated (and interesting) is that these different things all interact. **Everything is connected.***

Our brains and mental health

Our brain is where the processes responsible for our thoughts, emotions and awareness happen. Our brain is connected to the rest of our body by a network of nerves and cells called our nervous system. Information is sent by electrical impulses which travel along our nerves and change the amounts of different chemicals in our brain and body. These chemicals affect how we think, feel and behave.

Genes and mental health

Our genes are a template for how our brains and bodies will grow. We get our genes from our parents. There is no one gene that influences our mental health. There are lots of different genes involved and we don't yet fully understand how all of their effects add up.

Some genes give us an increased risk of mental health problems, which means it's good to be extra careful of looking after our mental health if we know family members have had problems.

BUT... it's really important to know that even if we have some genes which make us more likely to experience mental health problems, this doesn't mean we definitely will have a mental health problem. How our genes are expressed is affected by our environment: the places we live, the food we eat, the experiences we have, can alter which genes are expressed in which way. This interaction is called epigenetics.

Stress and mental health

Our mental health is affected by stress. Stress is the feeling of being under mental or emotional pressure.

Some stress is useful; it gets us doing stuff. Too much stress is unhelpful and stops us being able to do things.

Stress curve

One way of thinking about this is the stress curve:

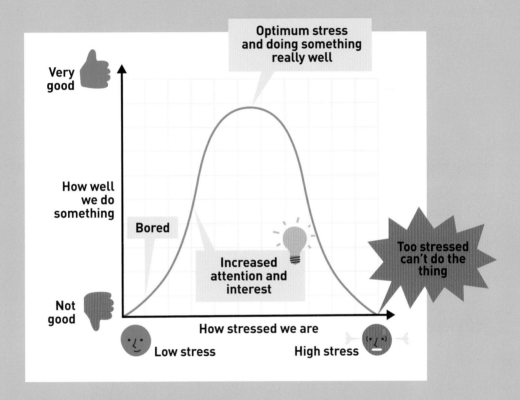

Where does stress come from?

Stress can come from all sorts of things. For example, schoolwork, tests or exams, moving home or school or other big changes, trouble getting on with our friends, arguments at home, or experiencing things like bullying and unfairness.

Sometimes things that seem like they are good can still be stressful – like doing really well at school, but then feeling a pressure to do well again – or getting a new friend, but then worrying about how much they like you.

Stress can also come from worries about the world around us, for example climate change or politics. It can sometimes feel like there's a lot to worry about.

Stress and discrimination

Sometimes the stresses we have to deal with are to do with other people's attitudes to us.

Discrimination is treating people unfairly because of who they are. Discrimination is bad for our mental health. Racism, sexism and ageism are all types of discrimination. What other types can you think of?

Sometimes people are discriminated against because of their sexuality. Fancying people who are the same sex as you doesn't mean you have a mental health problem - it's just about who you fancy! But, sadly, people who identify as gay, lesbian, bisexual or queer tend to experience more discrimination than people in straight relationships. People who identify as transgender also experience more bullying.

"Black men in Britain are ten times more likely than white men to be diagnosed with a psychotic illness … The reasons are complex, but discrimination and cultural differences do play a role."

David Harewood, actor

"I'm a queer, transgender poet. I first came out at school at the age of 12 and it wasn't always easy … I struggled with my mental health for a long time as a result, and I turned to poetry as a way to express everything I was feeling."

Mikey Barnes, activist, student and poet

How do you know if you are stressed?

We feel stress in our body as well as in our head. This is because stress hormones have physical effects. These are ways that our body responds to stress hormones like cortisol and adrenaline, which get us ready for fight, flight or freeze.

This is a response which we have inherited from our ancestors, in times when they would have been running away from animals like sabre-toothed tigers. It's our body's way of being ready to run away, fight or stay very still so we don't get eaten.

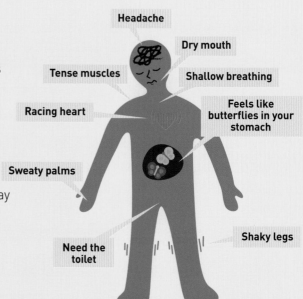

Headache
Dry mouth
Tense muscles
Shallow breathing
Racing heart
Feels like butterflies in your stomach
Sweaty palms
Need the toilet
Shaky legs

We don't have sabre-toothed tigers around anymore. Sometimes the 'tigers' we are worried about won't ever happen – they are just scary thoughts.

Having stressful thoughts that are around for longer mean those stress hormones stay around for longer too. This can be bad for us, not just because it's miserable to feel stressed but because our body's stress response is supposed to be short-lived. So the more we can do to help ourselves calm down, and stop ourselves behaving as if a worry is a tiger, the better.

THINK ABOUT

We all have a different "stress signature" in our body - places we notice stress (I tend to get a tight jaw or tense shoulders). Where do you notice stress in your body?

We all have stressful things that happen. They can fill up our stress bucket. Most people also have ways of punching holes in the stress bucket so it doesn't overflow. These things can include talking to people who understand us, looking after our bodies with healthy food and sleep, having a balance of things we like doing as well as things we work hard at, trying to be kind to ourselves and asking for help if we need it.

Sometimes it's worth checking that the things that are punching holes in our stress bucket aren't accidentally funnelling some stress back in. Things like shouting at someone, ignoring work we have to do or shutting ourselves away and not talking to anyone, can all feel good in the short-term but may hurt us in the longer-term.

We can all manage a certain amount of stress, but when our bucket overflows things get too much.

Worries and stresses fill up our stress bucket

WORRIES AND STRESSES

STRESS BUCKET

Holes in the stress bucket are things that let the worries out

Watch out! some things we do accidentally funnel the stress back in!

THINK ABOUT

What things do you use to punch holes in your stress bucket? What do you do that makes you feel better?

My Experience

MARIANNE VAN DEN BREE

Marianne Van Den Bree is a research Professor from the School of Medicine at Cardiff University studying the development of mental health problems in children and young people.

What do you do?

I study why some children are more at risk of developing mental health problems. Some children are able to overcome even very difficult things that happen to them, and others may be thrown off track by what seem to be minor problems.

What has mental health got to do with the brain?

The brain plays an important role in who we are and how we think and feel. The chemicals in our brain change throughout the day and make us feel different feelings – such as happy or sad. Our genes play a major role in the structure of our brain, how parts of the brain are connected and how it works, including those different chemicals. We humans have over 20,000 genes in the cells of our body and these influence who we are and what we look like as well as our risk of medical problems, including mental health disorders.

In addition to genes, how we live our lives, for example the food we eat, the exercise we do, and how we are looked after by other people, affects our brains and our mental health too. We are learning more and more about how genes and the situations we live in affect each other.

Why are some people more at risk of mental health problems than others?

We know that the environment children grow up in matters. For example, being able to talk about your problems and getting help from your parents, siblings, friends or teachers can help you cope with difficult situations.

Our genes also matter. But it is not as simple as one single gene leading to a specific mental health problem. Research has told us that many genes play a role in this. Most of us have some genes that increase our risk of having a mental health problem. The more of these risk genes we have, the more the chance that we may develop a mental health problem.

It's complicated though! Some children may develop a mental health problem even though they have only few of these risk genes, whilst others may have many risk genes, but will never experience any mental health problems. This is because both genes and the way we live our life are involved in mental health problems developing.

What have you learned from your research?

I study children who are at very high risk of having a mental health problem, because they have specific genetic differences, which most other children do not have. They are also more likely to have physical health problems.

Studies of the brain have shown that its structure and how it works can be also different in these children. This shows us that genes affect the brain as well as our behaviour and physical and mental health.

It is important to remember that not all children with these risk genes have problems in all areas and some experience no difficulties at all. Other factors, such as stressful life experiences and lack of social support are also important.

Genes and how we live our lives both affect mental health in ways that are individual to each child. By working this out, it will be possible to give children better help in the future.

"We are learning more and more about how genes and the situations we live in affect each other."

WHY DON'T WE TALK MORE ABOUT MENTAL HEALTH?

How often do we tell the truth when someone asks us how we are?

Often people say they feel fine when actually they feel something else. Sometimes saying we feel fine even though we don't can make us feel more able to do things and this can make us feel better. It's a sort-of "faking it to make it" approach.

If this works, then great. It doesn't always work though.

Sometimes we might just want to keep how we feel private for a while. Which is okay, as long as it doesn't make us feel too lonely, and as long as we know we can talk to someone when we feel ready.

Other times we might think we should pretend to feel okay. Unhelpful ideas like "boys don't cry" and "strong people stay silent" can get in the way of being honest about how we feel.

When feelings get really big

Sometimes feelings feel so big that it can be hard to talk about them. We might worry that we will get really upset, or angry, or scared, and not be able to control what we do or say. We might worry things will just get worse if we talk. We might worry that our feelings are so big or weird that other people will feel scared of them.

"People are scared to talk about it, but they should be scared about not talking about it."

Prince Harry, UK Royal Family Member and Co-Founder of Heads Together, speaking about his own mental health ups and downs

When something is frightening or hard to think about we sometimes talk about it being like a monster, or as if it is something so different that it can't be anything to do with us. This might be why there are sometimes really mean words used about people with mental health problems. Words like "mad", "crazy", "insane", "psycho" and "mental" make everyone feel worse and they don't help to explain what's going on or make it any better.

THINK ABOUT

Are there any words you use or your friends use, even as a joke, that might make people think it's not safe to talk about how they really feel?

#mentalpatient

A few years ago some supermarkets in the UK had Halloween costumes for sale which said they were "mental patient" costumes. They were horrible costumes based on old-fashioned treatments and horror films. People were really cross that mental illness was shown like this and many of them posted pictures of their own faces on Twitter under the hashtag #mentalpatient to show that mental health is something everyone has and that anyone can experience problems.

Stigma

Stigma is when people view someone as being less good than other people because of something like mental health problems (or other things, like disability or skin colour or sexual preference). This usually makes the people who are being stigmatised feel really bad.

"As you grow you realise the ridiculousness of the stigma attached to it. Like, what? You just talk to someone about your problems."

Jay-Z, rapper, on talking about mental health

"I have never been remotely ashamed of having been depressed. Never. What's to be ashamed of? I went through a really rough time and I am quite proud that I got out of that."

JK Rowling, author

Helping each other

Talking to someone we trust when we feel strong emotions can be really helpful, so it's important that we help people feel that this is okay. We all have mental health, it's just part of being human. We need to look out for each other.

"[I]f you see somebody that's hurting, don't look away. And if you're hurting, even though it might be hard, go tell somebody and take them up in your head with you."

Lady Gaga, singer, on mental health

My Experience
CHAMIQUE HOLDSCLAW

Chamique Holdsclaw is an Olympic-Gold-medal-winning basketball player and mental health advocate.

Growing up loving basketball

I grew up in Queens, New York, and once I found my passion in playing basketball, you couldn't keep me off the court.
I played with the boys most of the time, I didn't have anything to prove, I just wanted to get better every time I touched a basketball. Once I got into high school, it felt like everyone knew me for playing basketball. It was an incredible feeling and when I was playing, I was able to ignore my mental health issues, such as terrible anxiety and depression which sometimes meant I couldn't get out of bed or leave my house for days.

Other people's reactions to mental health problems

Often my outbursts and episodes were explained away as teenage behaviour and my grandmother encouraged me to pray instead of seeking professional help. In the black community, I have heard countless stories of "praying away" physical and mental health issues and that God or religion is the only thing that can help. I think this attitude is unhelpful at best, and at worst it can be damaging or even dangerous, as it can make people feel ashamed of having mental health problems and prevent them seeking help.

Feeling ashamed of mental health problems

As I got older and played basketball in college and professionally, I was so embarrassed that I suffered from depression and that I had these manic episodes and anxiety. I didn't want the world to know. I had won an Olympic Gold medal, but I was too ashamed to get a mental health diagnosis. I was a professional athlete, but I was too scared to get professional help. I allowed this fear and shame to swallow me up for years.

The more I tried to run from it, the worse it would get and the harder it became to hide. Because of my silence and my illness, I tried to take my life. This was a turning point for me. I had to get help. I started seeing a professional to talk about what I was going through, but I was still very hesitant to accept that I might actually have a mental illness. I was sure that this was something that could go away.

What was it like to have a diagnosis?

When I was first diagnosed with bipolar disorder, it was unbelievable. I heard the words, but I wasn't able to identify with it. I was a professional athlete and not someone with mental illness. I tried different medications and for years still struggled

with the diagnosis and my mental health. Again, another episode sent me into a life or death situation. Was I going to finally accept that I had nowhere else to go but to do the work, regain my life, and take control of my mental health and recovery?

How things are now

Today, I am a mental health advocate and have had the incredible opportunity to share my story and journey with people all over the world. I especially love talking to young people because they are often curious and eager to understand their mental health which I was afraid to do when I was younger.

I had to get real about my diagnosis and understand what Bipolar II disorder was and what changes I needed to make in my life. I will never be cured of my mental illness, but it has now become an important part of my identity and allowed me to be more present and take my life one day at a time.

What I tell young people

I tell young people today who are faced with mental illness to take control of your own mental health as it is an important part of who you are, but don't ever let it define you.

" … take control of your own mental health as it is an important part of who you are … "

CAN YOU DIE FROM MENTAL HEALTH PROBLEMS?

You can always skip these pages if you think they might make you sad.

There are lots of ways that people with mental health problems can get help to feel better (some of them are described on pages 44 to 45). No one wants anyone to die from a mental health problem. Despite this, it does sometimes happen. This is really sad.

Feeling like there's no way out

Sometimes mental health problems can make people feel hopeless, think life is not worth living, or that people would be better off without them. It can feel like being stuck with no way out. These thoughts and feelings will pass, especially if they can be talked about with someone who cares, but sometimes they feel so strong that they make people try to end their life.

People who have tried this and survived have spoken about instantly regretting their actions. For example, Kevin Hines, who now gives talks to share his experience, said: "I realised I made the greatest mistake of my life."

"Your mind is a galaxy. More dark than light. But the light makes it worthwhile. Which is to say, don't kill yourself. Even when the darkness is total. Always know that life is not still. Time is space. You are moving through that galaxy. Wait for the stars."

Matt Haig, writer, from *The Humans*

Difficult thoughts and feelings

The mental health charity Young Minds estimates that 25 per cent of young people experience suicidal feelings at least once. Having these feelings or thoughts doesn't mean you will act on them. If you do have these thoughts or feelings, speak to an adult you trust.

Talking about difficult thoughts and feelings is really important for feeling less alone and being able to see another way through. Some services which help young people with these thoughts and feelings are in the back of the book.

> *"The world is full of wonderful things you haven't seen yet. Don't ever give up on the chance of seeing them."*
>
> J.K Rowling, writer

Even when people think that ending their life won't matter to anyone else, it affects everyone around them. Research estimates that 115 people will be affected by each suicide that happens.

Young men are more vulnerable to suicide. There are different ideas about why this is, but part of it may be that boys are often encouraged to keep quiet about how they feel. Not talking to other people can make problems seem unsolvable and stop boys getting the help they need.

> *"What are we saying to a boy told to "man up" or to "act like a man"? Often, we're saying, "Stop expressing those feelings." And if a boy hears that enough, it actually starts to sound uncannily like, "Stop feeling those feelings.""*
>
> Robert Webb, actor and writer

> *"It's not that you're weak or can't handle life. Sometimes you're stuck and life does that."*
>
> Stormzy, rapper, on depression

> *"Talking about it, looking after your mental health, admitting you need help, that life can be tough ... these are the TRUE definition of being "manly"."*
>
> Scroobius Pip, rapper

My Experience
CHINEYE NJOKU

Chineye has been a young carer of a parent with a mental illness for most of her life. She now uses her own past experiences to help other young people who have a parent with a mental illness. She is a CBT therapist (see page 44), advocate and public speaker.

Could you tell us about your experience of having a parent with a mental health problem?

My mother was diagnosed with bipolar disorder when I was born. Bipolar disorder is a type of mental illness that affects your mood - you can either feel very low or very high and over-active. This meant that growing up I had to look after my mother as well as look after myself. I struggled to balance the two sometimes. I have never been diagnosed with a mental illness but there were times where I struggled with shyness, worry, guilt and low mood. I also noticed that my own wellbeing was at times based on my mother's wellbeing.

During my early teenage years, I did not take out time to think about what I had been through, which would have helped me understand things better; I just got on with life. Luckily for me, I received help from a charity that supports families where there's a parent with a mental illness. I also had two teachers in both primary and secondary school that cared enough to find out why I was not taking part in school activities. They both talked to me and I was able to focus better at school.

Have you got any advice for the readers of the book?

Don't avoid your own feelings. It is sometimes easier to deal with other people's feelings than to face your own. You can understand and make sense of your feelings if you talk it through with someone and try to understand what has upset you. It is not unusual to feel like staying away from people when you feel down, but it is important that you share your feelings with someone you like and trust. If like me you also have a family member with a physical or mental illness, please remember that you don't have to look after them all by yourself. Helping your loved one can also include telling them to go and see their GP or take up help from local services.

"... it is important that you share your feelings with someone you like and trust."

My Experience
ALAN COOKLIN

I'm Alan Cooklin, a psychiatrist – a doctor who helps people with problems in their minds. I also help people with relationships.

What is your experience of helping when a parent or carer has a mental health problem (or mental illness)?

It can be pretty scary if your parent suddenly behaves in ways you cannot understand. It usually happens for lots of reasons, and you can't catch it. We set up the charity Our Time because children whose parents had a mental illness:

- did not get a proper explanation of what was happening to their parent
- often blamed themselves – even though that's not true
- often felt they were the only child living with mental illness in a parent
- had no one to talk to
- feared they were going to "catch" the illness
- felt ashamed of themselves and their family
- felt lonely and sad about losing closeness to their parent
- sometimes felt they must try to agree with strange ideas of their parent, which was bad for them.

Our Time helps to explain mental illness and link children with other young people in a similar position, and with calm grown-ups to talk to. Some things we have learnt:

- It is never your responsibility to make your parent well and you could not have made them ill.

- Try to find an adult you can trust to talk to. You must not feel you have to hide what is happening out of loyalty. That will be bad for you, and in the long-term will not help your parent.

- Get an explanation which satisfies your curiosity and keep asking until you really understand.

- Keep or make a group of friends, and join in school and other activities. If you have brothers or sisters, talk and try to plan together how to support each other.

My Experience
SUZI GAGE

Suzi Gage is a psychologist and epidemiologist at the University of Liverpool. She researches the link between recreational drug use and mental health. She makes the podcast Say Why to Drugs, co-hosted with Scroobius Pip (see page 27), and is author of the book Say Why to Drugs.

What is a drug?

The word "drug" can mean a few things. Drugs might be the medicines that we are prescribed by doctors, or given in hospital. But "drugs" is also a term for substances that people might take for fun. Some of these drugs are illegal, like cannabis or ecstasy, but alcohol, cigarettes and coffee are also drugs. In its broadest sense, a drug is something that temporarily changes the body. When we're talking about drugs that aren't prescribed, the effects are usually on the mind or brain – they might change how we think, or how we feel.

What have drugs got to do with mental health?

This is a surprisingly hard question to answer. We know that drug use and poor mental health are connected – when we look at groups of people that use drugs, there are higher levels of poor mental health, from depression and anxiety to rarer disorders like schizophrenia. In groups of people with poor mental health we see higher levels of drug use, including tobacco, alcohol and cannabis. But understanding what this connection means is more tricky.

Perhaps drugs increase the risk of mental health problems. Or it could be that people who are struggling with their mental health might be more likely to turn to drug use as a way to deal with their problems. Another option could be that earlier life experiences or even genetic factors might increase the risk of both, and the connection we see between drugs and mental health is just because of this earlier risk – it's extremely hard to tell!

One problem is how we investigate these links. We ask people to tell us about their drug use, and about their mental health – we measure what people choose to do.

The problem is that people who choose to use cannabis (for example) are different from people who don't in lots of other ways aside from their cannabis use (for example, they might have different personality traits such as being more impulsive). It could be these differences that are increasing the risk of poor mental health, and it can be hard to take account of them.

Do you have any advice for readers?

No drug use is without the risk of harm (legal or illegal) – and while we're not 100 per cent certain that drugs cause poorer mental health, it seems likely that they do from the evidence we do have. And we know that drugs have other risks too, including physical health harms and, for illegal drugs, the risk of getting a criminal record or even going to prison too.

We also think - from evidence we currently have - that drug use is particularly risky for children and teenagers, while the brain is still developing, and this could also help explain the link between drug use and mental health problems.

"We also think - from evidence we currently have - that drug use is particularly risky for children and teenagers, while the brain is still developing ..."

WHY DO WE SOMETIMES DO STUFF THAT MAKES OUR MENTAL HEALTH WORSE?

We probably all have some things that we like to do that make us feel good in the short-term, but don't make us feel so great in the longer term.

Like ... Have you ever eaten loads of something you really enjoyed but then felt sick afterwards?

Worries and stresses fill up our stress bucket

WORRIES AND STRESSES

STRESS BUCKET

Holes in the stress bucket are things that let the worries out

Watch out! some things we do accidentally funnel the stress back in!

Ways of coping

It is sometimes easy, especially if we're stressed, to get into using ways of coping that feel good in the moment but make us feel worse later on, or accidentally keep a problem going.

Remember the stress bucket? It's those coping strategies that are accidentally funnelling stress back in.

I've got a small example of this sort of unhelpful coping strategy. I drink loads of coffee when I feel tired. Short term it helps me stay awake (and is delicious) but it also makes me feel anxious when I have too much and it stops me sleeping at night (which makes me feel tired the next day).

THINK ABOUT

Are there any things you do that make you feel better in the moment but not so good longer-term?

WHAT CAN HELP US MAKE CHANGES?

It can take a while to change and use different coping strategies. I don't know about you, but if someone tells me to stop doing something I usually want to carry on doing it.

Two researchers, called Prochaska and DiClemente, worked out a model of how we tend to approach making a change in what we do. They thought it takes us a while to even realise that we need to make a change, and then it takes us even longer to think about whether we really want to. We then need to plan how we will make a change, to give us the best chance of succeeding.

Even after we've made a change it takes us effort to stick at it. It's normal to slip up and go back to old habits.

Take my habit of drinking too much coffee … according to Prochaska and DiClemente, once I realise I need to cut back I might still take a while to mull over whether I really want to. Maybe I make a plan to only have one cup a day. I might prepare by cutting back gradually, then try to stick to only one cup. I might have a day when I drink five cups again, kind of like a coffee relapse. With the stages of change model this is fine, and to be expected. It just means trying again to give it up, if that's what I still want.

If you are trying to make a change don't be hard on yourself if you have a slip up. It's totally normal and human. Just try again.

Trying to build any changes into a daily routine and remembering what the point is of making the change can also be helpful.

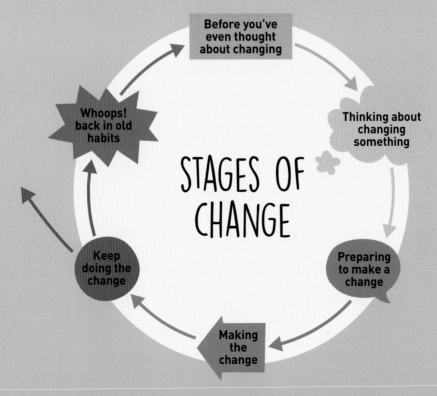

My Experience
FISKY

Fisky is a poet, rapper and public speaker. He runs a monthly event called Mind Over Matter which encourages talking about mental health through spoken word poetry, hip hop and song.

What do you wish you had known about mental health when you were growing up?

When I was 16 a lot of things happened that made me very sad. Mental health wasn't spoken about much back then and none of my friends understood how I was feeling. I didn't think I was allowed to feel sad so I did a lot of things to try and make myself feel better and bury those feelings. None of the things I did were good for my body or my mind.

If I could speak to the younger me I would tell him, "the way you're feeling is normal. The things you've been through are not easy to deal with at 16 years old and the next few years are going to be very difficult. But things will get better." I'd tell him to write more and that the way he's feeling doesn't make him weak. It makes him human.

If someone had told me this, things might have been a lot easier to understand and it wouldn't have taken me so long to move on and be happy again. Taking care of your mental health is just as important as your physical health.

What do you think spoken word has to do with mental health?

Any kind of writing, poetry, hip hop, short stories, keeping a diary or just writing your thoughts down on a page can help you understand how you're feeling and why you're feeling that way. Getting all the jumbled up thoughts out of your head so you can read them makes things a lot easier to understand. That's all poetry is. Writing your feelings on a page. Poems don't have to rhyme.

Spoken word poetry is poetry you perform. This is also very helpful and can make you feel better. Words are very powerful. When I first started performing I was nervous because I hadn't said these things out loud to anyone before. When I did it, a whole new world opened up and I met people that understood and supported me. Finally, I didn't feel alone anymore.

What makes you worry and what makes you feel better?

Whenever I worry or feel sad I pick up a pen and write down how I'm feeling. I don't think about it too much. I don't try to be clever or use lots of big words. When I feel like I've got everything out of my head I re-write it a few times maybe changing words or sentences here and there to make it a bit more creative. When I've finished, I know I've created something that didn't exist before, which makes me feel good.

Other than writing I like to spend time with friends, go out to eat, go for walks or days out, go swimming or create and perform poems and songs with my friends. All these things help me feel better.

What advice would you give young people?

Sometimes, when you feel sad or worried it can feel like it's only you that feels this way. You aren't alone. We all have these feelings from time to time. Speak to your parents, teacher or someone you trust and let them know. Holding things inside like I did for such a long time isn't healthy and can lead to a lot of problems.

Writing changed my life and I'm much happier now. I'm also able to help other people who might be going through the same things I went through when I was 16.

If you can't find the words. Try writing it down.

"Any kind of writing, poetry, hip hop, short stories, keeping a diary or just writing your thoughts down on a page can help you understand how you're feeling and why you're feeling that way."

WHAT'S SOCIAL MEDIA GOT TO DO WITH MENTAL HEALTH?

*S*ocial media just means websites and apps we use to be social. Most social media sites say you should be over 13 to use them, and there are some worries around the best ways for young people (and adults) to use these sites.

Why are people worried?

Connecting with people can be good for us, so why do some people worry about social media and mental health? Social media is relatively new. We are still finding out about its effects. Did you know that in the 1500s many people thought that the invention of printed information was "confusing and harmful", because suddenly more information was available to more people in the form of the printed word. It's unlikely anyone would be given a hard time for reading books today.

> *"The evidence suggests that social media can make things worse for some people. But it can be a source of help too. It's good if someone who cares about you (a best friend, a parent) knows what you're doing so they can check that the effects are positive not negative."*

Sonia Livingstone, Professor of Social Psychology at the London School of Economics

Professor Sonia Livingstone, social media expert, says it impacts our mental health in at least four ways:

1. "If we use social media when we're feeling unhappy or worried or depressed, we might find it hard to deal with the nasty things some people say to each other, so it can make us feel worse.

2. "At the same time, if we use social media to let our friends know when we're feeling bad, they can be really supportive and encouraging, making us feel better.

3. "If we look on social media for something negative or harmful, then the algorithms that select what we see can offer us even more negative content, making us feel worse.

4. "Sometimes we just use social media to block out the world, forgetting that we'd be better off sharing how we feel with someone we trust who could help."

Like lots of things, it's all about how we use it.

Hard to get a break

One tricky thing with social media is that it's 24/7, so it's hard to get a break from it. If someone is being mean it can feel hard to escape. Using social media might also stop us meeting up with people, or having "downtime" when we're not using our phone or computer. It also might affect our sleep.

Things that help if you are using social media:

1. Sleeping in a room without phones.
2. Unfollowing people and not searching for people or things that make you feel bad.
3. Having breaks from social media.
4. Trying not to use it to compare yourself to others.
5. Trying not to make decisions, get into arguments, or post pictures that you're unsure about online, especially when you are feeling unhappy or worried.
6. Remembering things you post stay online or can be screenshot.
7. Keeping a list of things that you find helpful or happy on social media.
8. Finding a way of using social media that suits you.

THINK ABOUT
Can you think of more top tips?

WHAT WAYS OF THINKING HELP OUR MENTAL HEALTH STAY HEALTHY?

Can we exercise our mind?

Yes! We can practise thinking in different ways. When we think, cells in our brain communicate with other brain cells. The communication pathways between brain cells get stronger if they are used more. So the more we think something the more likely it is we will think it. If we make an effort to think in a certain way then it actually gets easier the more we do it.

What ways of thinking help or don't help?

There are some styles of thinking which we all get into that aren't very helpful.

Ruminating is when we think over and over and over something that has already happened and we end up feeling bad about it.

Did you know that it's called ruminating because it's like what cows do when they ruminate on grass? Chewing it over and over to digest it!

Worrying is when we think about something that hasn't even happened yet and all the possible things that could go wrong, and try to solve them in advance. A little bit of worry can be helpful - too much can make us feel really bad.

Other styles of thinking that aren't that helpful include black or white thinking - where we oversimplify choices; mind reading, where we think we know what someone else is thinking; and snowballing, where one bad thing happens and we turn it into something much bigger by thinking about all the possible things that are going to happen now.

Everyone thinks in these different ways sometimes, but if you catch yourself doing them lots you might want to try something different. When I catch myself ruminating – chewing over and over a thought in a way that makes me feel worse – then I try to think about something else instead, like focusing on what is going on right here and now.

What's helpful?

Noticing the good stuff

Making a decision to be more aware of the good stuff can sound too easy, but noticing the little things each day that we enjoy can make a real difference to how we feel.

Mindfulness

One way of practising noticing the small things each day is called mindfulness. Mindfulness doesn't mean emptying your mind or doing lots of stretching. It's about paying attention in a kind way to whatever is happening right now. That includes your thoughts, your surroundings and what you're doing. It means not getting caught up in worries about the past or the future.

"Being alive and knowing it."

Jon Kabat-Zinn, founder of a talking therapy called mindfulness based stress reduction

"Yesterday is history, tomorrow is a mystery, today is a gift - that's why they call it the present."

Master Oogwe in Kung Fu Panda

Being kind to yourself

It's easy to get into telling ourselves off in our own head, or reminding ourselves of things we should have done or ways we wish we were better or more like someone else. The way we speak to ourselves can be really nasty. How often to you say "well done" to yourself? How often do you tell yourself off for not doing something well enough?

"Instead of being our own worst enemy, with practice, we can learn to become our own best friend."

Mary Welford, clinical psychologist

Try this

Next time you catch yourself having a go at yourself in your own head, try asking yourself this: "What would I say to a good friend?" Try saying whatever you would say to them, to yourself instead.

WHAT THINGS CAN WE DO TO HELP OUR MENTAL HEALTH STAY HEALTHY?

Exercise

There is good research to show that being active helps us feel happier. Even better if it's something we find fun. I mostly go swimming, to a yoga class and sometimes for a run or to a dance class. It's nice to do different things.

> *"I love boxing. It really helps me and makes me feel strong."*
>
> Ellie Goulding, singer, on exercise and mental health

Eat healthily

More and more scientists are discovering links between our guts and our brains. Eating healthily gives us enough energy to feel good, and having the right nutrients keeps our brains healthy as well as our bodies.

Doing what we love

Doing things that are fun and that we enjoy for the sake of them is important.

Doing what we feel proud of

Doing things we find hard but we feel proud that we have done give us a sense of achievement.

Doing what matters

Noticing what we think is most important in life and trying to do things that fit with that is helpful too. This is called living in line with your values.

Sleep

When we are tired we tend to be more emotional, irritable, sad and also hungry. It's harder to concentrate if we haven't slept enough. Top tips for sleeping well include not watching screens (like TV or phones) too close to bedtime, trying to have a regular sleep routine (the time you go to bed and wake up, and the things you do before bed) and trying to do relaxing things just before bed. Writing things down in a notebook can help with nighttime worries.

Spirituality

For some people their religion or spirituality is really important to them feeling good.

Where we are

The places where we spend time can affect our mood. Green places, like the countryside or parks, can be good for our mental health. Or notice where you feel happiest and spend some more time there.

Who we spend time with

Spending time with people who are nice to us, who want us to be happy, and who care about similar things is good for us. Spending time with people who aren't kind to us can make us feel blue. Sometimes this can even tip into bullying - which is really bad for us. If you're worried this might be happening to you try to talk to someone you trust about it.

Being assertive

In friendships and other relationships it's important we try to say what we want and say if we feel unhappy about something the other person is doing. This can take practice. At first it might come out as if we are being snappy or being mean. Don't be discouraged if this happens - just keep trying to talk calmly about what you want.

Being kind to others

This might sound obvious, but if we're cross, or hungry, or tired, or scared or sad, it can be easy to be mean, or not to make the extra effort to be kind. We know that treating people unkindly is bad for their mental health. It also usually makes the person who is being mean feel bad. Connecting with other people in a kind way is good for us as well as them.

Pets

Having a pet around can be really good for making us feel happy and relaxed.

Hugs

Hugs are good for our mental health too, as long as the person you are hugging doesn't mind.

Creativity

For some people having a creative practice is really important: writing, drawing, singing, dancing, playing an instrument or listening to music. Reading can help us feel less alone too, especially if we read about someone who is having similar experiences to us. What do you do that makes you feel good?

Try this

Try to do one thing every day for the next week that you feel proud of, and one thing that you enjoy when you're doing it. They can be really small things. Try to keep track of them and see how it makes you feel.

My Experience
CHRISTINE RAI

Christine Rai is an artist from New York City. She has a webcomic called "Yeah It's Chill" where she explores a range of topics and everyday stresses loosely based on her own experiences, including worries that many people recognise and also worry about.

How do you choose what to draw about?

Most often I draw comics based on things that I've experienced recently. Sometimes I think back to memories that are funny or interesting or painful and I draw those. Other times I draw things that are inspired by museums trips, travel, things I've read or seen, or conversations with my loved ones. One of my favourite things about drawing and creating is there are no rules to what you can make, you can always do what you want.

Feeling feelings

From when I was quite young up until very recently I beat myself up about emotions I felt that weren't happy. Anytime I wasn't happy, I'd get upset about being unhappy and it added shame and guilt on top of whatever else I was feeling. Now I know and remind myself that all emotions come and go and none of them are bad or good, I don't have to feel good all the time. Feeling bad and feeling all ranges of emotions is perfectly fine, normal and human. We go through cycles and seasons just like the rest of nature. Remembering this helps me during times when I don't feel sunny. Rain and storms are necessary and important too.

When I'm sad, it feels less like a small rainstorm and more like a hurricane. When I'm worried it's less like a windy day and more like a tornado. I used to be upset with myself about this and jealous of people who seemed better at being a person than me. But now I know I am here to be the best me I can be, I can't be anyone else. And I know these feelings will come and pass and I'm gentle with myself during these times.

I remind myself that I have gone through hard times before and everyone throughout history has too, we've all lived through them.

"Feeling bad and feeling all ranges of emotions is perfectly fine, normal and human."

Having a tool box of things that help

I know my anxiety is a thing that will always live with me so I developed a tool box to make things easier and I'm always adding to it. I wouldn't do anything else without having the supplies I need to do it the best way, caring for my mental health is the same.

Hiding painful emotions doesn't make them go away, and I don't need to hide them. Talking about them and asking for help changed my life. Now I know what I need to feel safe and I do those things.

What do you find helpful?

One thing that helps me when I feel like my emotions are bigger than I can handle is to imagine that I'm a big, sturdy, strong tree with my long roots firmly and deeply planted in the ground and I have branches that fan out and go high up into the sky. When I'm feeling anxious, I feel like I could float away into space. I close my eyes and take one deep breath. Then I imagine I'm the biggest tree, firmly planted. This helps when it feels like my body is too small to hold all the emotions I feel, like a cup with too many feelings spilling out and all over everything.

WHAT SUPPORT IS AVAILABLE?

Now there are different sorts of support available if mental health starts to feel not-so-healthy. The main thing is finding something you find helpful.

There are a lot of different types of talking therapies. You can ask your GP (doctor) to refer you, or sometimes you can refer yourself.

Cognitive behavioural therapy (CBT) helps people think about the links between their thoughts, feelings, body and behaviour. Often changing one of these changes the others. You and the therapist work together on what you think the main problem is. The CBT model is drawn out below.

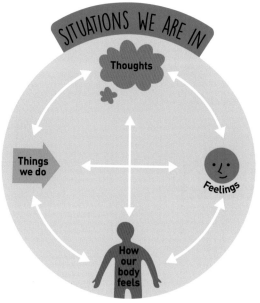

It's important that you get on with whoever you see. You can always ask to change.

Family therapy is another sort of talking therapy - it helps families to speak together about difficult things and try to find ways out of unhelpful patterns.

There are other sorts of talking therapies too.

There are also creative therapies that use the arts, like music, art, drama, dance, writing or play to help someone understand and think about difficult feelings. These therapies can be especially helpful when it feels impossible to talk about something directly.

"Sometimes it is not easy to talk about feelings and it can be helpful to use images to communicate and think about feelings and thoughts."

Valerie Hartland, Art Therapist

Medication

There are medicines available to help with different types of mental health problem. They work by affecting the chemicals in the brain. For young people medication is used very carefully, because the brain is still developing. Medication can be used at the same time as talking therapy, it doesn't have to be one or the other.

How do you know which treatment works?

There is lots of research looking into what works best for different problems and different people. You can talk to your GP about this and there are also guidelines based on research. In the UK these are called the NICE guidelines. NICE stands for the National Institute for Health and Care Excellence.

It's worth remembering that not having any studies doesn't mean something doesn't work, it just means no studies have been done yet. Studies showing something is either helpful or unhelpful are definitely worth taking notice of though. You can ask your GP or the person you are seeing what the evidence is for what they are offering.

Who works in mental health?

Lots of different people work in mental health. Some of their job names sound very similar but they do different things. They often work in teams together.

Some of them are:

Mental Health Nurse: a trained nurse specialising in mental health, who looks after people experiencing mental health problems, especially in times of distress or confusion.

Occupational Therapist: helps people to be independent and to find or get back to doing things that are meaningful to them.

Social Worker: helps to keep people safe, makes sure people can access resources and helps people to speak up for what they want.

Support Worker: helps people day to day with things that are difficult, listens to the person about what they want help with.

Psychiatrist: a medically trained doctor specialising in mental health problems. They can prescribe medication as well as being interested in what might have brought the problem about.

Clinical Psychologist: I'm a clinical psychologist. We try to help people make sense of what's going on for them and use talking therapies which have been shown (by research) to be helpful for mental health problems.

It's always okay to ask the person you are seeing what training they have had to do their job. Many professionals are registered or accredited which shows you that they have had a good enough training.

THINK ABOUT

People have different ideas about what treatments are best for mental health problems. Who do you think should be involved in deciding what treatment somebody has?

45

WHAT NEXT?

I hope you know more now about what mental health is, why it's important and where it comes from.

Quick quiz

1. What is mental health?
2. Where does it come from?
3. Who has it?
4. What are your three top tips for looking after mental health?
5. What's one thing you can do for a friend to boost their mental health this week?
6. What's one thing you can do for yourself this week to make yourself feel good?

Mental health problems are just one end of the spectrum of mental health. We can think about taking care of our own and others' mental health even when we feel good – maybe especially when we feel good.

What if I'm worried about someone I know?

It's caring to worry about someone. You can't make someone feel better or make someone seek help, but you can be there for them and show them the information in this book if you think it might be helpful.

If you're worried, it's important to talk to someone else. If you're worried about sharing a secret you can do this without saying who the person is.

What if I'm worried about me?

The first thing is to talk to someone you trust, like a teacher or a family member or your GP or school nurse. If you want to talk to someone you don't know there are helplines listed on page 48, along with websites and books that might be useful. It might help to use this book to have more conversations about how you and the people around you are feeling.

Look after yourself

I hope you will remember to take care of yourselves. It's not selfish to look after yourself, it means you will be able to look after other people better too.

I hope you'll try some things from this book to see if they can be useful. Find what works for you and keep being kind – to yourself as well as others.

GLOSSARY

advocate a person who puts a case on someone else's behalf – someone who speaks up for someone or something.

algorithms a set of rules followed by a computer.

anxiety feeling worry or fear to an extent that gets in the way of living your life.

behaviours the way we act, things we do.

bipolar disorder a condition that affects people's moods, where they swing from one extreme to another (very high to very low).

brain an organ in our central nervous system that controls our body, thoughts, feelings and behaviours.

depression a mental illness which includes experiences of feeling very low, hopeless, lacking energy and not getting pleasure from things

eating disorders a collection of different diagnoses involving unusual ways of eating or exercising that can interfere with someone's life, e.g. anorexia nervosa, where people eat very little, or bulimia nervosa, where people eat more than usual but then make themselves sick or take laxatives. These conditions aren't just about food, they also involve strong feelings and cause a lot of distress.

environmental relating to or arising from a person's surroundings.

epidemiologist scientist who studies illnesses within large groups of people.

epigenetics the study of biological mechanisms that cause genes to be expressed differently in response to differences in the environment.

gene a unit of DNA that controls the development of one or more traits and is the basic unit by which genetic information is passed from parent to offspring.

genetics the branch of science that deals with how we inherit physical and behavioural characteristcs, including physical and mental health problems.

mental relating to the mind (the part of us that has thoughts, feelings and awareness).

obsessive compulsive disorder a mental illness which involves being very preoccupied with particular worries or thoughts (obsessions) and feeling the need to do certain behaviours (compulsions) because of those thoughts, to a degree that interferes with someone's life.

physical relating to the body.

post-traumatic stress disorder a reaction to a trauma lasting for a long time after the trauma has happened. Includes feeling very anxious, experiencing thoughts or images about what happened, and avoiding talking about or thinking about what happened. Usually accompanied by shame or self-blame and can really interfere with someone's life.

psychosis a mental illness which includes a range of different experiences, all of which involve a loss of contact with reality, e.g. hearing voices that aren't there or having strong beliefs that aren't true. The experiences get in the way of someone living their life.

recreational drugs drugs taken for enjoyment rather than to treat a medical condition.

researcher a person who carries out academic or scientific research.

schizophrenia recurrent experiences of psychosis and also "negative symptoms" which are things like loss of pleasure, loss of motivation, finding it hard to think clearly.

self-harm when somebody intentionally damages or injures their body. It's usually a way of coping with or expressing overwhelming emotional distress.

spectrum a range of different positions between two extreme points.

suicide intentionally causing one's own death.

FURTHER INFORMATION

Book list

Reading Well is a UK charity which puts together helpful book lists on different subjects. They have two book lists for young people about mental health:

https://reading-well.org.uk/books/books-on-prescription/young-people-mental-health

Websites

CALM stands for the Campaign Against Living Miserably and is a charity founded by rapper Professor Green that aims to help men with their mental health.

https://www.thecalmzone.net/
0800 58 58 58

Childline is a UK-based helpline for under-19s
https://www.childline.org.uk/
Freephone 0800 11 11

Inspirited Minds is a faith-based charity aiming to help people with mental health problems, particularly those from a Muslim faith.
https://inspiritedminds.org.uk/about-us/who-we-are/

Kids Health has more information about the brain.
https://kidshealth.org/en/kids/brain.html

Mind is a UK-based mental health charity.
https://www.mind.org.uk/

Mind-Ed has information about children and young people's mental health.
https://www.minded.org.uk/

Mindfulness in Schools project is a charity teaching non-religious mindfulness in schools.
https://mindfulnessinschools.org

Our Time helps to explain mental illness and link children with other young people in a similar position, and with calm grown-ups they can talk to.
https://ourtime.org.uk

Papyrus is a UK youth charity for the prevention of young suicide.
https://papyrus-uk.org/
0800 068 41 41

Samaritans is a UK-based helpline.
https://www.samaritans.org/
116 123

Sikh Your Mind is a UK-based charity trying to improve knowledge in the Sikh community about mental health problems and how to help.
http://sikhyourmind.com/

Stonewall is a UK-based charity for lesbian, gay, bi and trans people.
https://www.stonewall.org.uk/

Young Minds is a UK-based charity for children and young people's mental health.
https://youngminds.org.uk/
They have different numbers on their website for young people and for parents.

INDEX